Leading in *Chaos*

Insights to Lead through the Storms

Updated Edition with Executive Leadership Insights

I. J. Neal

Former Deputy Mayor |Co-founder Onyx Rising

ISBN 978-1-64492-662-8 (paperback)
ISBN 978-1-64492-663-5 (digital)

Christian Faith Publishing
Meadville, PA
www.christianfaithpublishing.com

Revised Edition 2026

Printed in the United States of America

I dedicate this book to Willie Sam Neal, Jr. He was my biggest cheerleader, my champion, my confidant, my friend, my protector and my husband for forty-seven years. He was with me through every one of the situations I present in **Leading in Chaos.** This is the first major project I have completed without him.

Love you forever Sam.

Foreword

By Kelli Lester

I have a confession to make.

When I. J. first handed me the manuscript for the original edition of Leading in Chaos, I read it the way you read something written by someone you love — nodding along, proud of her, already planning what I would say when she asked what I thought.

Then I got to Chapter Four. And I stopped nodding.

Not because something was wrong. Because something was exactly right — and it hit closer to home than I expected. I. J. was describing a leadership moment I had lived through myself. The paralysis of a team that had stopped trusting its leader. The silence in rooms that used to be full of ideas. The way dysfunction doesn't announce itself loudly; it just quietly drains the energy out of a place until one day you look around and realize the best people have already started looking for the door.

I had been in that room. I had been that leader — or at least, I had stood beside leaders who were navigating it with nothing but instinct and hope. And here was I. J., putting language to something I had spent years trying to describe.

That's what this book does. It names things.

I. J. Neal has spent more than three decades in environments where the chaos was real — not metaphorical. As a Deputy Mayor navigating the politics of a major American city, as an executive leading human services programs through crisis after crisis, as a business owner who built multiple companies from the ground up, she has been in rooms where the stakes were not theoretical. The frameworks in this book were not developed in a classroom. They were forged under pressure.

What makes this revised edition different is that I. J. has done something harder than writing a book the first time. She has gone back in. She has reexamined every insight through a new lens — the lens of what organizations are actually facing right now. The post-pandemic workplace. The leadership vacuum left by rapid, forced change. The managers who were promoted for what they could produce but were never equipped for what people actually need.

She has made an already honest book more honest.

I want to tell you something about I. J. that the bio on the back of this book won't capture. She is the kind of leader who walks back into hard situations by choice. Most people, when they've earned the right to step back, step back. I. J. steps forward. I have watched her sit with executives in the middle of organizational crises and not flinch. Not because she doesn't feel the weight of it — but because she has learned, the way you only learn through experience, that chaos is not the enemy of great leadership. It is the condition under which great leadership becomes visible.

That belief is on every page of this book.

I am I. J.'s niece. I am also her business partner, her Co-Founder at Onyx Rising, and — on my best days — her thought partner when the problems are hard and the answers are not obvious. I say this not to suggest I am unbiased. I say it because I think it matters that I have seen her lead, not just heard about it. The woman who wrote this book is the same woman who shows up in the room. There is no gap between what she teaches and how she lives.

That kind of integrity is rarer than it should be.

You'll read about I. J.'s work from another perspective in the following pages — from someone who witnessed her leadership at the highest levels of federal government. I'd encourage you to read both. They describe the same woman.

What I hope for every reader of this book — whether you are a CEO, a principal, a team leader, or someone who simply finds themselves in the middle of something that feels uncontrollable — is that you will find in these pages what I found that first time I sat down to read it. Not just tools. Not just frameworks.

Recognition.

The recognition that what you are navigating has been navigated before. That it is survivable. That there is a path through — and that the leaders who find it are not the ones who pretend the chaos isn't real. They are the ones who learn to lead anyway.

You are holding a guide written by one of those leaders. **Rise.**

Kelli Lester

Co-Founder & Leadership Strategy Partner

Onyx Rising

Praise for Leading in Chaos

If you are so fortunate in your lifetime, you may meet one or two individuals who strike you immediately as exceptional. Those amazing few, who exude confidence, possess insight and good judgment, and, most importantly, have a good heart (and a slightly cynical good nature) can change the world. I. J. Neal is one of those treasured few I have had the pleasure, not just to meet but also to work with over 30 years of our long careers. She is a trusted and esteemed colleague, and one of the best Administrators of a major government department I have known!

I. J. and I began our careers working in the Indianapolis office of the Prosecuting Attorney. She was so successful there that she was recruited to take on the equivalent department in Washington, D.C. – a department twice the size as Indianapolis' in staff and budget and also light years behind it in every other measurable way. I. J. was bound and determined to bring positive change, and under her leadership she turned it into one of the best in the country.

If I had known what that job would entail, I am not sure I would have encouraged I. J. to take it on – although, knowing I. J., I never doubted her ability. The first few weeks and months on the job, I. J. and I talked every day after work.

"You won't believe what happened today!" would often be her opening refrain. And what she had to deal with, indeed, defied belief.

Leading in Chaos brings back so many memories! It is a tale of woes and wiliness that defies belief, but I can attest that every bit of it happened and is truly related. Read it and learn how a dedicated and determined manager can prevail over seemingly insurmountable obstacles. Or just read it for the sheer pleasure of following along on an incredible journey with a young and determined woman who just won't give up.

—Donna Bonar,
Deputy Commissioner,
Office of Child Support Enforcement, U.S.
Department of Health and Human Services

In three years, I watched I. J. turn the dumping ground that was the District of Columbia Office of Child Support Enforcement Division into the Yale of child support programs. The DC Child Support Division went from last place to number 10 on the federal performance scale in two short years. The "dumping ground" became the upper echelon of agencies within the federal and district government due to I. J.'s extraordinary management skills.

Just as Rome was not built in a day, she had her work cut out for her from the first day she walked into the department. Her stellar reputation had preceded her and those opposed to change had prepared to wreak havoc and chaos. Enduring threats, Inspector General investigations, attempted political intimidation and union grievances; it took faith, prayer and a tiny core team of colleagues that would support I. J. in the endeavor to bring about positive change.

All of the events depicted in **Leading in Chaos** are true. I should know. I worked side by side with I. J. every day. I am Diane. Read about my role in Chapter 5.

—Sharon Diane Stokes,
Former Administrator, District of Columbia,
Department of Human Services, Office
of Child Support Enforcement

I. J.'s life and career are an inspiration. She has been a trusted friend and colleague for more than thirty years. I was an astonished and admiring witness to many of the vivid episodes and management insights she offers in this book. I. J. is strategic by nature and has the courage of a lion, yet she is truly and faithfully compassionate qualities that are abundantly evident in the stories she tells in this book. They are also the qualities that inspired dedication and loyalty among employees who became a team during her tenure as a department director for the City of Washington DC. I. J.'s deliberate actions led a beleaguered staff from an unimaginably chaotic environment to a productive setting for success. Truthfully, the challenges she accepted with that position appeared insurmountable to her friends and colleagues. Then we watched in awe as her strength and equanimity created space for change and triumph. Her leadership inspired enthusiastic commitment among her staff who were demonstrably grateful and bereft at her departure. I have grown immeasurably from I. J.'s counsel over the years, and now this book offers everyone the benefit of her hard-won experience and sage advice.

—Carolyn Kastner
Former director of state and local poli-
cies, Center for the Support of Families
Curator Emerita, Georgia O'Keefe Museum

Contents

Preface

I have been blessed to hold a variety of positions in my career in and out of the government. From my first job as an advertising clerk at a local paper (where I cut out ads all day and pasted them on cardboard) to serve as vice president in two Fortune 500 companies. This is MY story of my time in Washington DC as a department director for the District of Columbia. It is a narrative tale of my actual experience in the complex political and social environment of DC government while managing a department of one hundred twenty civil servants for the DC Mayor Marion Barry. Every one of the events is true however, the names of the individual staff members have been changed.

My story is not meant to scandalize the DC government or anyone associated with it, but rather to share the lessons I learned during those tumultuous years.

I believe that people are inherently good, and that everyone has worth. I hope this book and the *Leadership Insights* that I shared from my career will inspire managers in every type of business. Perhaps it will help you when things get really rough and, if work ever becomes mundane, perhaps you will find my story to be at least entertaining.

I learned to believe in people and in myself from my parents. My father offered me my first lesson in business. "There is no such word as CAN'T" is what I heard from my father on an almost daily basis. Every time my siblings or I said "I CAN'T," we were told, "You can do anything! It may not come quick and it may not be easy, but if you persevere, you will succeed."

My mother's favorite saying to us was taken directly from the Bible. "In all things get an understanding" (Proverbs 4:7). It means "Ask lots of questions. Make sure you are clear in what is being communicated, and act accordingly."

I am the second of eight children born to an African American working-class family in the Midwest. Educated in public schools and universities, I used every opportunity afforded me to improve my life. We grew up in what would be considered today "abject poverty" caused by too many mouths to feed with too little income.

Despite the rough start, I graduated from college and was happily married to my high school sweetheart for forty-seven years until his untimely death. I had risen rapidly in my career before the move to Washington DC. As you read the following pages of my years in DC government, more than once you may ask, "Why didn't she quit and go home?" Believe me, I thought about it more than once. I didn't quit because I had never been exposed to quitting. I NEVER saw my father or mother giving up no matter how difficult the challenges!

I witnessed my father be humiliated by circumstances beyond his control. He never bowed his head. He never made excuses and he never quit! My mother would pray and pray and pray but never gave up! Not quitting was ingrained in me so deeply, my spirit would not allow it!

My siblings and I laugh about it today. We each know that no matter the odds or how difficult things appear, none of us would ever say "uncle" and simply throw in the towel! That is not how we were raised.

I always enjoyed a challenge in the workplace. My forte was to build something positive out of the ruins and to effectively deal with difficult people.

Early on in my career came one of my toughest work challenges.

I was a secretary at a book publishing company while attending Indiana University at night. My immediate supervisor was a survivor of the Holocaust. She told such harrowing stories of terror that she endured and was a profound inspiration. She was not bitter, even though she had lost her entire family and personally suffered unimaginable atrocities.

She recommended me to become the executive secretary for the managing director of marketing and promotions. It was a substantial promotion.

In his off-hours, the managing director was an officer in the John Birch Society (the same as the KKK). At first, I thought, *Somebody's got jokes!* A young black woman working daily for a racist? But then I thought, *Why not? He will learn through me that all his stereotypes are wrong.*

I talked it over with my supervisor who encouraged me to go for it. BUT WAIT! First, I had to, as my mother had taught me, get an understanding.

During the interview with the managing director, he actually called me a "pickaninny" as he outlined his expectations. I didn't think I had ever felt such rage but pictured in my head an episode my father had recently endured, so I held my tongue.

After he finished I looked him straight in the eyes and said, "Respectfully, Sir, I also have some expectations."

He looked like I had shot him!

I said to him, "While I know that our political views are extremely different, my only concern is how you will treat me on a daily basis. I expect that you will not refer to me as a *pickaninny* or any other derogatory term again. My name is I.J. I expect you to always treat me with respect and that includes by not using any racial slurs in my presence. You will never ask me to do anything immoral and you will respect me as a person of faith. I will, in return, give you the best work product I can possibly deliver. I will be on time, dependable, and I will always represent you and this department in a professional manner." In short, I assured him that I would live up to the expectations he had outlined as his executive secretary, and more if he would honor my expectations as well. WHAT? I was twenty-two years old.

Where did I find the strength to talk to him that way? From my mother. I had to get an understanding.

I got the job as executive secretary. I learned a lot: how to disagree in a respectful manner; how to make my case with facts, not with emotion; and how to deal with difficult people. Most importantly, I learned that every bad decision in the workplace is not racially motivated or biased.

I developed my own barometer and asked myself a series of questions before I acted. I could not say truthfully that I was never called the "N" word while in this position. What I can say is that the managing director never used it in my presence or in earshot! Unfortunately, in my naivete I thought that my excellent job performance would change the director's views about African Americans.

In the end, while we both honored our mutual under-standing, the director remained a racist. He simply believed I was the exception to his general rule!

I think I learned the most about how NOT to manage people from my next job at Indiana Bell telephone company where I was a telephone operator. I took this job strictly for the money. By then, I was married and had an infant son.

The most egregious of the many, many rules were the necessity to ask permission to go to the restroom. Some of the (male) managers thought it was funny to deny this request from female employees. Needless to say that type of management behavior was toxic. In fact, it led to a labor strike that lasted several months. Ironically, it was the very managers that created the hostile environment that had to answer the calls for the length of the strike. I heard that they too had to ask to go to the bathroom! The Communications Workers of America union sued Indiana Bell and won after several years. I was asked if I wanted my job back. By then, I had moved onward and upward!

The job that really propelled my career was working for the Marion County prosecuting attorney, Stephen Goldsmith. He is the smartest person I have ever worked with before, then, and since! He was all about performance and excellence. No politics or partisan favors clouded his workplace. I was promoted eight months after I started working for Steve.

I was asked to manage a large unit within the prosecuting attorney's office. At the time, it was an overlooked and underperforming unit.

From my first day in the new position, I knew that the staff had been demoralized, and they needed a leader who believed in them and would support them.

I told the staff, "Give me all you got, and within one year, people will be transferring from other units of the office to work with us!"

That was exactly what happened! I kept getting promoted, kept learning, and I was always hungry for more! I NEVER asked for a promotion. I NEVER asked for a raise, but they both kept coming. I simply did each job to my own personal standards, knowing that if I could meet my own standards, my performance would be rewarded.

Eliminate "Can't" From Your Leadership Vocabulary

In today's high-pressure, understaffed, politically charged work-places, leaders who default to "can't" signal defeat before the work begins. Resilient leaders reframe impossible-seeming mandates as constrained problems to be solved. Replace "we can't" with "here's what it would take." This shift — from paralysis to possibility — is what separates effective executives from those who merely manage decline.

Seek Understanding Before Action

Toxic environments thrive on ambiguity, rumor, and assumption. Before reacting to a crisis, a difficult employee, or a political threat, invest in deep situational understanding. Ask more questions than you answer. Clarify expectations in writing. Leaders who act on incomplete information in chaotic organizations routinely make defensible problems into expensive ones.

Invest in People, Even the Most Difficult Ones

Research consistently shows that leaders who maintain belief in their employees' capacity to grow — even those who have failed "repeatedly — create cultures of psychological safety that outperform fear-based environments. This is not naivety; it is strategic. People who feel seen and given a genuine second chance frequently become an organization's most loyal and productive contributors.

<hr>

Chapter 1
TVs, Fish Fries, and Sex

Ms. White asked, "Are YOU going to tell Marsha she has to take her TV home?"

I replied, "Ms. White, you are the manager, so YOU are going to tell her!"

Another one of the managers chimed in, "Well, I.J., while we at it, SOMEBODY ought to stop them from frying fish in the office every Friday! Whole fourth floor smells like fish!"

WHAT? I was the new director of a District of Columbia government agency; two weeks on the job. The first Friday on the job I was at an all-day director's meeting. This encounter was my first substantive management meeting.

Oh, I had convened introductory meetings and one-on-one meetings, but this was my first all managers meeting for the department. I had gotten an earful. Through personal observation and one-on-one meetings, I found that several staff had portable TVs at their desks and spent more than their lunch hour looking at TV. YES! Looking at TV.

I also found out about a "secret" office that was used for all sorts of illicit behavior from using drugs to an infamous couch that was said to be the place for sexual encounters. Lord, what had I gotten myself into?

I had left a job as the administrator at the Marion County prosecuting attorney's office where I had developed a great staff and worked hard to make our office *the best in the nation*. We had received numerous federal, state and local awards. It was an office that was fun to work in. My boss, Stephen Goldsmith, was one of the brightest people I had ever known.

I moved to Washington DC for what I thought was the opportunity of a lifetime. It *was* a lot more money, a much bigger budget and staff, more autonomy, but LORD! TVs, fish fries, and sexual encounters all in one office? I began to wonder whether I had made a serious mistake; so much so that I wanted to call my old boss and ask if I could have my old job back, but I didn't.

I gave the order to get rid of all the TVs and informed the staff that fish fry Fridays were over. I immediately required the staff to sign in and out for lunch, and warned that anybody caught looking at TV would be subject to disciplinary action. My assistant oversaw the conversion of the "secret office" to a workspace and the infamous couch went to the dumpster!

My mother was my closest consultant. I would talk over problems with her and she would pray. It seemed that whatever she asked God, he did it. Well, I told her about my week—all of it. She immediately started praying over the phone, worried about what I had gotten myself into and worried for my safety. I must admit that this little sheltered girl from Indianapolis (nap town) was scared. I had been in management for nearly a decade, but I had never been in an office situation like this before. Little did I know there was much worse to come!

It was the practice of all the managers to lock their offices when they left for the day. I didn't question this practice. I just followed it. On Friday after the new operating procedures had been relayed to all staff, I locked my office and headed home for a much-needed weekend of relaxation.

Monday morning, I got to my office and the lock was broken. The door was wide-open, and the office was totally destroyed. There was a dent in the plexiglass window that looked like it had been made by a bullet! My prize possession: a painting signed and presented to me by one of my mentors, had been ripped off the wall and smashed with a hammer. Glass was everywhere, and the painting was destroyed.

A flood of emotions went through me: fear, anxiety, but most of all ANGER!

I left my office and marched to the desk of the office busy body, the one who would make sure the message was spread far and wide, and I said to her, "You tell the motherfuckers who did this that they should have left me the hell alone! I was about to go back home! NOW I'M NOT GOING ANYWHERE!"

I called the chief of police and asked him to send over an officer to investigate. He responded by sending six police officers. I asked him to personally make a quick visit the same day. I called Mayor Barry, who had hired me, told him what had happened, and asked him to make a quick visit. I called the city council representative and asked him to stop by, and lastly, I called the court administrator and asked one of the judges to make a visit.

Everyone showed up! What was remarkable about this response to my call was that I had met most of them only two weeks before! With the help of my assistant, I coordinated each of these visits for optimal visual effect. I did NOT clean up the office and I kept the door open for all of these meetings. I orchestrated a show of force for two reasons: (1) to tell the staff and the perpetrators that I was NOT alone. I had the backing of the power in the DC government. These individuals were highly respected and the fact that they would take time out of their busy day to show up for me meant I must be *all right too*; and (2) it was to instill a level of fear in the perpetrators and the entire staff.

I never talked to the staff about the incident (but they knew). I never asked them who did it (but they knew). I wanted the guilty parties to be on edge for as long as possible. I wanted them to feel uneasy, and most importantly, I wanted them to be ostracized by the rest of the staff. That was exactly what happened! The atmosphere in the office changed! It gave me the breathing room to start to implement lasting changes and improvements.

Map the Power Landscape Before You Need It

Leaders who wait until a crisis to build relationships with key stakeholders find themselves without allies when it matters most. In your first 90 days, identify and connect with every power broker, formal and informal — elected officials, department heads, community representatives, and institutional leaders — before you need their support. These relationships are your organizational insurance policy.

Ask for Help Strategically and Without Shame

Leaders in toxic or high-pressure environments often mistake self-sufficiency for strength. In reality, the ability to mobilize a coalition when under threat is an executive superpower. When you face a crisis, identify who has a stake in your success and activate them. The leaders who weather institutional attacks are those who have built visible, reciprocal relationships long before the storm arrives.

Chapter 2
Dump on Me!

"Don't you know, this department is the government dumping ground?"

My department had one hundred twenty staff! I answered, "No, I was not told that when I was hired!"

I had never heard of a *government dumping ground*. What I found out later is that some state governments have a place to transfer troublemakers and misfits; an agency out of the way usually buried deep in the lower levels of the organizational chart.

My department had been that place until federal legislation mandated performance standards along with incentive funding. One hundred twenty misfits and troublemakers? New expansive federal legislation had been enacted requiring major changes in all procedures. Performance standards were tied to financial incentives for success with severe penalties for failure.

The profile of the DC department was being elevated. National attention was being placed on the new policies and expectations were high. Brand new private sector businesses were being created to help states meet the federal mandates.

Suddenly the federal government was picking up the tab for sixty-six percent of all operating expenses, and if we met the performance standards, the federal government paid one hundred percent of the operating expenses for the program!

I was selected from a national search tasked to clean up the problems and implement the new federal mandates. I actually turned the job down the first time. I had a glimpse of the amount of effort that would be required. The table for success was not adequately set AND it was not enough money!

In reality, I had NO idea how deep the challenges would be, but Mayor Barry seemed determined that I was the right person. He called and said, "Give us another chance. Let me show you how committed we are to making this work!"

Of course, I said okay.

I was picked up at the airport in one of Mayor Barry's cars, whisked through town directly to his office where I met with him one-on-one, his entire staff, including the city administrator, who became a great ally, and all other government department heads—police department, economic development, health department, etc. I was really impressed by Mayor Barry telling every one of them that they had to give me *all the assistance required* to help me succeed.

I went through a series of meetings that day to understand how to leverage the different resources of the city government, and he offered a salary that was nearly double my current salary!

He had set the table. I just needed to decide if I wanted to stay for dinner!

As I was being driven to the airport for my return home, I looked over at the Jefferson Memorial so stunning at dusk and said to myself, *How can I NOT do this? The city is beautiful. It is our nation's capital.*

The challenges will be great, but the rewards will be greater.

"Show them what you're made of, girl!"

I went home to begin the transition.

Conduct Rigorous Due Diligence Before Accepting a Turnaround Role

The most costly leadership mistakes begin with insufficient discovery. Before accepting a high-risk role — especially a turnaround in a politically complex environment — verify the specific conditions required for success: decision-making authority, resource access, executive alignment, and a realistic timeline. Ask for the organizational history, personnel files summary, federal audit records, and an honest assessment of the political landscape. Leaders who skip this step often inherit both the dysfunction and the blame.

Compensation Must Reflect the True Scope of the Risk

Executive leaders in toxic or underperforming organizations absorb enormous reputational, emotional, and professional risk. Accepting inadequate compensation signals — to yourself and to the organization — that the difficulty of the work is not fully acknowledged. Negotiate compensation that reflects the real challenge, not the idealized version. You cannot sustain a multi-year turnaround if you are already resentful of the terms.

Chapter 3
You Can't Leave!

"Steve, I'm giving my thirty-day notice. I got a fantastic job offer to head a department in DC, but I have a favor to ask."

"What do you mean you are giving notice? YOU CAN'T LEAVE," said Steve with anger. "I'm not giving you more money if that's what you're trying to do!"

It was the first and only time I had seen him angry. I had worked for him for eight years, respected him, and thought of him as a mentor, but at that moment, I felt he was treating me like his property. No free will for you I. J. *Just do what I tell you!* In my mind, his response and tone was racial, and it hurt. But I used my racial barometer and concluded that his reaction was to one of his key staff catching him off guard with a resignation.

I walked out of his office. If I had stayed, I would have said things that could not be unsaid. I needed to cool off and I figured he did too.

After I cooled down, I wrote a heartfelt and professional resignation letter. I recounted several of many accomplishments under his leadership. I also recommended my replacement and closed by saying I would be asking for a favor.

I made an appointment to see him the next day, and before I could get all the way in the door, he apologized. I laughed and said, "I know. You are going to miss me!"

He laughed and said, "I WILL give you a raise if you stay!" But he knew my mind was made up.

"What's the favor?"

Mayor Barry was under a criminal cloud. He had not been indicted, but one of his key aides had been. There were rumors that criminal charges against Mayor Barry were imminent.

Mayor Marion Barry was brilliant but considered an arrogant man to those in the federal government who oversaw the DC budget and management. The District of Columbia is not a state and has no senator or representative who can vote in Congress to protect its interests.

DC can tax its residents but not diplomats or the tens of thousands of commuters, who flow in and out of the city every day. None of the huge federal buildings and vast properties within the district is subject to local property taxes. Thus, the district has to rely on Congress for substantial funding from the federal government, and Congress can impose its judgment and laws notwithstanding local laws passed by the DC city council.

Previous DC mayors had paid considerable deference to Congress, especially during budget hearings.

Not Mayor Marion Barry. He was raised in the days of Jim Crow. He had been a leader in the civil rights movement and a lifelong activist, and no white man was EVER going to tell him what to do, nor was he going to kiss ass to get what he felt the district was owed.

I asked my boss, Stephen Goldsmith, who was acquainted with the federal prosecutor to find out if there was a federal case pending against Marion Barry, and whether or not he was likely to be indicted.

The last thing I wanted to do was to move to DC only to see my new boss indicted as soon as I got there.

Steve said, "Give me a day or two. I'll ask." True to his word, in a couple of days I heard, "ALL CLEAR!" Now I had to tell the staff.

I started with the managers and was really surprised by their reaction. Not one of them congratulated me, "That's a great opportunity. I am happy for you." It was the same as it was with Steve. "You can't leave. You belong here. How can you leave us?"

Everyone seemed to be looking at my departure strictly from his or her point of view. How were office operations going to change? Who would replace me? How would it affect them? I was so surprised!

These encounters told me a couple of things: First, the staff had become comfortable that I would always be there to solve the problems, pick up the pieces, and make everything better; and second, they were much too dependent on me.

I had to reassess my management style. Had I unintentionally made myself indispensable? This scenario was not good for me or those who worked for me. If I ever had any doubts about leaving, their response to me meant I had enabled dependency and it was time to leave!

Apparently, I did leave a pretty big hole! Can you imagine how I felt when two people replaced me? Even after I left, I was getting phone calls telling me how bad everything was, and that, I had to come back.

When I returned home to complete the move to DC a couple of weeks later, I took several of the managers and staff out to lunch and said unequivocally, "I am NOT coming back. Would you if you were making more money, had a bigger staff, bigger budget, more authority, and live in a beautiful new city? Work with my replacement. Make the office what you want it to be!"

Finally, requests for me to come back ceased. The message was sent and received!

Trust Your Internal Signal — and Act On It

Leaders in demanding environments are frequently the last to acknowledge their own fatigue, stagnation, or misalignment. Your instincts about when a chapter has closed are almost always correct. The danger is in negotiating against yourself — accepting a raise, a title, or additional resources to stay in a role whose ceiling you have already reached. Keep your own counsel. When your gut says it is time to move, honor it.

Protect Your Vision From Others' Emotional Needs

When you lead a high-performing team or a successful turnaround, your departure will trigger genuine grief among those who depended on you. That grief is real — and it is not your responsibility to resolve it at the expense of your career. Leaders who allow the emotional needs of their teams or colleagues to override sound career judgment often end up resentful, stagnant, and less effective than if they had moved on. Compassion does not require self-sacrifice.

Chapter 4
Drugs

"Call 911!! John has OD'd in the men's room!" John was on my staff and he had just overdosed on heroin in the office bathroom unconscious with the needle still in his arm. He had overdosed on heroin in the workplace during working hours. In the office, five hundred feet from his desk! The paramedics reached him in time and revived him.

My reaction: I was glad he was alive, but I was FURIOUS.

I began writing up his immediate termination. Where I came from, if you were caught using drugs on the job it was grounds for immediate dismissal. Where I came from, such behavior was not tolerated. BUT WAIT! Not here. Not in DC. Not in this unionized office.

Using drugs was considered an illness, and addiction is a disability requiring a referral to the employee assistance program. ARE YOU KIDDING ME! No suspension, no disciplinary action, whatsoever?

The union representative told me about John's rights. I responded, "What about the rights of all the other employees in this office who may be jeopardized by his behavior? What about trying to maintain a safe and respectful environment for everyone? What about free will and personal responsibility?"

The union representative said that I could terminate him, but if I did, know that he WOULD get his job back. Termination would mean mandatory arbitration. It would take about two years with all the appeals, but HE WOULD GET HIS JOB BACK with back pay.

An examination of my personal value system went into overdrive. I liked John. He was smart and personable, but I was responsible for all the staff. I had a job to do. I had to change this toxic environment, and I had to ensure that this department retained its federal funding!

I decided to terminate John. Before I did, I talked to Mayor Barry and to the city administrator. They both told me the same thing. They agreed that using drugs in the workplace should be grounds for immediate termination, but they both said in DC presently it was not. However, they both told me it was my decision. I was hired to manage the department and I had the authority to do what I thought was best. I terminated John effective immediately.

BUT WAIT! This story has a sequel.

"I.J., Paul just OD'd at his desk! We just called 911. They are on the way!"

This was less than thirty days after the incident with John.

Once again it was heroin and, once again the paramedics arrived in time to revive Paul. This time, however, there were extenuating circumstances. No immediate termination for this one. NO WAY! He was the nephew of a very powerful advisor to Mayor Barry.

Mayor Barry said, "NO. You can't fire him."

I understand politics. I know that politics can protect the connected and sometimes crucify those not connected. It was not fair, but it was the reality. To make matters worse, the local news organizations (newspapers, radio, and television) found out. The Metro Section of the newspapers read; "Employee overdoses in DC government office." "Rampant drug use in DC government offices."

Guess who had to talk to reporters and explain what happened? Guess who got called on the carpet by the federal government oversight agency wanting assurances that my department would turn around? You guessed it! ME! All alone.

I had to defend the agency. I had to defend the rest of the staff who was doing the best they could every day! I had to ask myself why I was going through this. I did not have to. I could go home. I did not have to take this shit! But I could not quit. I had to see it through.

Once again, my mother's prayers worked. This chapter had a happy ending. Paul was put on medical leave and then assigned to another agency. The shock of losing his job caused John to go into rehabilitation and kick the habit. He did get his job back.

It was twenty-eight months later. By then, the office was rolling. Moving up on the federal performance scale from fifty-second (only Puerto Rico and the Virgin Islands were lower) to tenth.

I welcomed John back. We even had a small celebration. I personally escorted him to his desk afterward. He became one of my staunchest supporters.

Lead From Your Values, Not Just From the Rulebook

In dysfunctional organizations, the rules are often written to pro-tect dysfunction. Leaders who allow procedural constraints to override clear ethical obligations forfeit their moral authority — and their team's trust. Know your non-negotiables before a crisis forces you to improvise them. When policy and integrity conflict, act from your values and be prepared to defend that decision with facts. Leaders who hold the line on standards, even when it is costly, build the credibility required for genuine organizational change.

Maintain Focus on Outcomes When the Environment Tries to Derail You

Toxic workplaces generate an almost constant stream of crises designed — intentionally or not — to consume a leader's attention and prevent meaningful progress. Develop and protect a clear set of organizational outcomes (metrics, milestones, performance standards) that remain visible regardless of the chaos around them. These anchors allow you to demonstrate progress to skep-tical stakeholders and give your team something stable to orient toward when everything else feels unstable.

Chapter 5
Troublemakers and Misfits

I had been on the job for about ninety days, and I had used most of my time assessing the strengths (and weaknesses) of the staff.

My conclusion was that it broke down as follows: About one third of the one hundred twenty employees were highly skilled, motivated, professional, and ready to embrace change; about one third were mediocre. They would do the job satisfactorily and would "go along to get along." Then there were the rest who were truly the troublemakers and misfits that I had been warned about (chapter 2).

Many of the people in this last group were actually quite smart. They knew how to work the system and had been doing it for years! Some of them were politically connected, and therefore, thought they were untouchable.

The best and brightest of the staff was my executive assistant, Diane. It is the absolute truth that all of the good that happened in the department while I was there had her name attached; and to the bad that happened, Diane contributed to the solution! We were a great team because our strengths were different. While I worked building partnerships outside the office, she was the rock inside the office. Her knowledge, understanding, and (not least of all) her connections within DC government were numerous; and we used them all on our road to success. We not only worked together closely, she became one of my closest friends. There were others, of course, who showed incredible skill and fortitude during my tenure. I am eternally grateful that they bought into the vision I had for the agency and used their skills on a daily basis to make it a reality.

But those troublemakers and misfits—suffice it to say, that they worked overtime to wreak havoc and destruction. The staff in this troublemakers and misfits category was collecting a government check making approximately $35,000 per year to $70,000 per year. With my Midwest values, I couldn't understand their lack of work ethic. Some of them did not even show up for work regularly.

In one instance, the staffer had been on disability leave for three years! After I inquired, it turned out she was working another job but collecting her full salary from the DC government every month! Another one was making more than the maximum for his pay grade, approximately $70,000 a year. He showed up every day, signed in, went in his office, closed the door, and read the paper and books all day long. He was a Ph. D. I learned later that he had been instrumental in helping one of the council members who got elected and apparently felt he was entitled to a patronage job for life. But there were three that were so destructive words cannot sufficiently describe them.

Looking back, the first one Janet was probably bipolar (unmedicated). She would come to work highly agitated one day and depressed the next. Her appearance and personal hygiene were terrible—uncombed hair, wrinkled clothes, unmatched socks, big and run-over shoes and she even smelled. She threw fits in the office, argued with staff, and would get in a verbal fight with anyone near her. Her behavior was not confined to her unit. She would go through the office cussing loudly, challenging anyone who looked her way. Her behavior took up a lot of my time. I would send her home. I would try to counsel her. There was something about her that I saw beyond her bad behavior. She was super smart! She was out of control most of the time, but when she was acting correctly, she was unstoppable. She was great at math and she could figure out complex problems.

One day, she came in to my office while Diane and I were having a meeting. She was crying hysterically and said, "My baby needs to be born. My baby is dying." She could not be consoled.

Then standing in my office, she pulled down her pants, reached into her vagina, and pulled out a doll about a foot long! Needless to say, Diane and I were appalled.

After recovering from the initial shock, Diane called an ambulance. Janet spent several weeks in the hospital and in a mental health facility.

Janet, like so many deeply troubled individuals, had a backstory.

While she was on medical leave, I learned that some unspeakably bad things had happened to her and it was no wonder she had become mentally unstable.

When I received word that she was well enough to return to work, I asked, cajoled, pleaded and finally ordered one of my best managers, Sandra, who was a devout Christian, to take Janet under her wing. I reasoned that the structure and calmness that Sandra exhibited daily would be good for Janet. It worked!

Under Sandra's guidance and with the medical help she needed, Janet excelled. She became one of my shining jewels. She applied for a promotion to another agency about a year later and got it. I saw her years later, and she was still doing well.

Then there was Calvin. He was an attorney, and his position was a policy analyst. But the job he excelled at was character assassination both inside and outside the office. He would make up lies and spread them everywhere. Because he was a policy analyst, his reach was far beyond my department. He worked with the corporation counsel, with our federal government liaisons, department of economic development, and numerous other agencies. He was shrewd and devious; and it took me several months to discern his true character.

Unlike Janet, Calvin was impeccably dressed every day. At first glance, you would have said that this is a young man who had it going on, but underneath that well-pressed monogrammed shirt was a diabolical heart. He spread the rumor that one of the women in the office was a prostitute, that another was dying of an incurable disease and could not perform her duties, that members of the staff were stealing money, and I knew about it. (This one resulted in an investigation by the DC inspector general's office. Of course they did not find anything.)

He and another staffer decided they did not like one of the managers who was tough but fair and decided they would accuse him of rape! Calvin really knew how to work the system. He poisoned my relationship with another department head.

To this day I do NOT know what he said or how he did it since I thought I had a very good professional relationship with this colleague. I learned later that my predecessor had tried to fire Calvin but had been unsuccessful. Calvin concocted a story that resulted in my predecessor facing disciplinary action himself. I watched my back around Calvin.

But I had not known pure evil until I met Jennifer! She was a big muscular woman who bullied through intimidation and fear. EVERYONE was afraid of her, including me!

At our first meeting only days after I was hired, she came into my office and said, "I know Mayor Barry, and there is nothing you can say or do to get me fired! I can do what I want to you and anybody else in this office, and nothing will happen! I thought I would warn you that my job and yours, if I want it, is mine! So don't fuck with me and I *might not* fuck with you!"

With more bravery than I felt I told her, "The day Mayor Barry tells me I can't fire your ass, if you give me a reason to, is the day I go home! Go tell Mayor Barry that!"

She stormed out of my office, but that was only the beginning. She attacked a staffer in the office that was suffering from breast cancer, deliberately hitting her in the affected breast and laughing telling her she was going to die. I learned that there were numerous similar instances involving Jennifer. How long had this been permitted to go on?

Apparently, Jennifer had been transferred to and from numerous other governmental agencies by managers who were too worn out to try to fire her. She was the kind you just wanted out no matter how or at what cost.

By now, it was obvious to me that I had to make staff changes if there was ever going to be sustained improvement. I knew it would take too much time to discipline and eventually fire approximately forty people, so I went to Mayor Barry and to the city administrator with a plan. I asked them to allow me to transfer half of them to other agencies. I made promises of increased collections and federal incentive payments if I was given the freedom to implement the federal policies rather than tie up HR with disciplinary actions. They approved the plan with the caveat that I would be able to transfer a maximum of fourteen people. I made the list. The first seven were easy. No contest. Jennifer was at the top! The last seven were a game of "Is this one worse than that one?" Were there previous personnel actions that might allow for justifiable termination in a short period of time if there were future infractions? Could I live with the behavior, and if I did decide to keep someone, how would it affect the staff morale and overall office performance?

Calvin was NOT on the list. He had not yet shown his true colors. I just did not know how bad he really was until much later.

It only took one day for me to come up with the list of fourteen. I submitted it to the city administrator whose task was to find other agencies for their transfer. To the amazement of everyone around me, especially my peer managers, the entire process only took about a week. Nothing like a mass transfer such as this had EVER been done before!

Sadly, staff was simply accustomed to people doing horrible things without repercussions. The good ones were used to working in a toxic environment. To them, the small changes—no Friday fish fry, no TVs, structure, communication—already implemented made the job immeasurably better. They didn't expect much more. They could not really see the agency being great. For me, I could not see anything but great!

When Facing Impossible Choices, Choose Decisively and Move

Toxic environments are engineered — intentionally or by neglect — to paralyze leaders with impossible options. Accepting that no available choice is perfect is not resignation; it is executive maturity. Select the best available option, document your reasoning, communicate it clearly, and move forward. Leaders who delay decisions in chaotic environments do not avoid problems — they compound them. Decisiveness, even with imperfect information, is a leadership act.

Know Who to Develop and Invest Deeply in Those People

Not every employee in a dysfunctional organization is a lost cause — and treating them all the same is a strategic error. The most effective turnaround leaders identify the employees with genuine potential (even hidden under difficult behavior), invest specifically and substantially in their development, and build those individuals into the nucleus of a new culture. Simultaneously, they recognize that some employees are not capable of or interested in change, and they act accordingly. Your energy is finite. Direct it where it generates the greatest return.

Chapter 6

Smooth Sailing?

"I.J., now that you have been able to transfer out the worst of the troublemakers, it should be smooth sailing!"

My management staff was delighted, and it *was* smooth sailing for about thirty days!

One day, a disgruntled bank employee who had been fired from a bank just half a block away from our office went back to the bank with a gun and killed several people, including the manager and assistant manager, several tellers, and a couple of customers. It was all over the news, and everyone was talking about it. Security had been increased around the area. We were all on high alert.

The very next day after the shooting, a staffer ran into my office and said, "I.J., JENNIFER IS ON OUR FLOOR! SHE'S WALKING AROUND THE OFFICE LOOKING CRAZY!"

I'm not going to lie, I was scared shitless.

Diane ran into my office. We locked the door and called the police. Then I looked out my office window where I saw my 6'4" 230-pound muscular brother walking across the street toward the office. I had made plans to have lunch with him and he showed up right on time. I told Diane, "We don't have to be scared now. My big brother is here! He will take care of Jennifer if she gets out of hand."

Well, Jennifer left before the police showed up without hurting anyone and without encountering my brother. She had made her point. It was just another indication of her ability to intimidate and generate fear! I could only hope that she would never return, but we stayed on high alert!

Resolved Problems Can Return — Build Durable Safeguards, Not Just Solutions

One of the most dangerous leadership assumptions is that a resolved problem stays resolved. Disruptive employees who have been managed out, transferred, or disciplined may return — physically or through surrogates who carry on the behavior. Effective leaders in toxic environments institutionalize safeguards: clear behavioral policies, documented procedures, trained managers who can respond independently, and external relationships (legal, HR, law enforcement) established before they are needed. One decision does not equal durable change.

Chapter 7
Secret Conversations

Diane, James, and I were in my office to have a candid discussion about James's chronic and long-standing failure to do ANYTHING to contribute to our operations. It was time for action.

"James," I said, "I cannot allow you to continue to get a paycheck every month without doing any work!"

"I.J., I paid my dues. I sacrificed for the people in this government and this job is how I am being repaid!"

"James, I am assigning you this project." I handed him the write-up of the project with dates for all of the deliverables. "I am going to go over it with you, and if there is anything you don't understand, let me know. Diane is taking notes, so that we don't have any misunderstanding about what is required."

I went through the assignment and the due dates and asked if he had any questions. Silence. He took the paper and walked out of my office.

The first deliverable was due in five days. I sent him an email reminding him of the due date two days before it was due. No response.

The day after it was due, I sent another email telling him it was late. A little later, I saw him in the hall on the way to the restroom which was the only time he came out of his closed and locked office door, and I told him that he had missed the due date for the first deliverable. Again, I was met with silence.

Ten days after the due date of the first deliverable and three days after the due date for the second deliverable, I wrote up a disciplinary action for failure to do work assigned to him. I gave it to him, and again, I was met with silence. Ten days after that, I suspended him for failure to do his job. For good measure I also had a new lock put on his door so that he was not able to get in. I had a feeling that he might ignore this suspension notice as he had every other directive I had given him. He did not ignore it. I got a call from the chair of the District of Columbia City Council. The conversation unfolded like this:

COUNCILMAN: Hello, I.J. We have not met, but I am Councilman Jones, chair of the DC City Council, with budget oversight authority over your agency. Don't tell anyone about the conversation we are about to have.

Diane and my operations manager were in my office when I took the call. I mouthed to them, "STAY HERE." And I began to repeat and respond to everything he said.

ME: Is there a reason you don't want me to tell anyone about this call?

COUNCILMAN: This is just between you and me. I understand that you have suspended James Johnson. I want you to rescind this action and get him back to work tomorrow.

ME: I repeat this for the benefit of Diane and the operations manager.

COUNCILMAN: Yes, that is what I said.

ME: Councilman, I will be happy to send over the file so that you can see for yourself that the action is justified.

COUNCILMAN: *He became highly agitated.* I don't need to see the file. I WANT HIM REINSTATED IMMEDIATELY!

ME: I understand that you want him reinstated, but I can't do that. Don't you want to know what he did?

COUNCILMAN: *yelling.* DO YOU KNOW THAT I CAN CUT YOUR BUDGET? I CAN MAKE YOUR LIFE HELL. IN DC, YOU ARE EITHER WITH US OR AGAINST US. IF YOU ARE WITH US, YOU CAN KEEP YOUR JOB, YOUR HUSBAND CAN GET A JOB, I CAN EMPLOY YOUR ENTIRE FAMILY, BUT YOU MUST DO AS I SAY.

ME: Councilman, I appreciate your position, but I would not be able to look at myself in the mirror if I rescind it. James deserves this suspension.

The Councilman hung up on me. I must say that I was visibly shaken. I had not ever experienced a politician's attempt to use his power in such a way. Approximately one week later, the secretary to the council chairman, who was a friend of Diane's, called her and said, "Hey, I see your department is scheduled for an oversight hearing in front of Chairman Jones' committee next Monday, and the press has been invited. What's up?" I knew what was up.

The councilman was going to extract his revenge in a very public way. Despite the rules of the council that said the agency must be notified of a council oversight hearing at least ten days before the scheduled meeting, we did not get notice! His plan was to humiliate me, and by extension, my office in front of everyone. If he was successful, I would either be fired or be so embarrassed I would resign.

I felt defeated for the first time. I DID call home. I called my mother first. Then I called my old boss, Steve Goldsmith, and asked if there was a job available. (I was ready to throw in the towel.)

He said, "Give me a couple of days, and I will pull something together." That really helped.

The third call I made was to my friend in the federal office. She was the only person I knew before taking the DC job. She said, "I.J. Turn this around on him. Everyone knows the incredible improvements you have made in that office! I'll mobilize the federal officials to come and testify on your behalf." She was on to something.

Diane called her friend, the secretary to the council chairman, and asked how to get people on the list to testify. She told us. Diane contacted several of the people we had recently helped and asked them to testify on our behalf. I called the court and asked the chief judge if he felt comfortable talking to the council about the progress the department had made in a brief period of time. Mayor

Barry just happened to stop by that day. (He was good at surprise visits all over city government.) I told him about the phone conversation with the councilman and about the pending oversight hearing. He said "Don't worry about it. I'll handle it."

But I was worried. I knew that Mayor Barry could not control the council and especially this councilman.

The day came. I looked at the list of people scheduled to testify, and EVERY ONE OF THEM was a person testifying on our behalf! I walked in the room with my head held high. All local television stations and local print media were there. Some of those troublemakers and misfits were also in attendance. BUT WAIT. The chief judge and three associate judges were there. The director of the federal office and four of her key staff were there to support us and counter any allegations of poor performance. Six people we recently helped were there. These were single mothers struggling to provide for their families. My beautiful staff was there in force. Our supporters outnumbered those against us 10–1. The place was packed!

The councilman called the meeting to order and gave this opening statement (I will never forget it):

> I.J., you have a lot of friends in this city! I got
> a number of calls from people asking me
> why I was picking on you. I told them it was
> just the opposite. I am taking this opportu-
> nity to highlight a part of DC government

that works; that has risen from the ashes in the short period of time you have been here, to become one of the nation's best!

REALLY?

The chief judge's panel was first to testify. Each of the judges painted a very stark before and after picture. Case preparation for court hearings had drastically improved, and the testimony from our office attorneys was stellar. They were always prepared and professional. There was also high praise for my management staff and for me.

Next up was the director of the federal office. She testified about the three days she had spent in our office shadowing my staff immediately before she accepted the federal job. She said my staff was exceptional, that everyone she encountered was professional, that my managers were personable and gracious. Then she praised the dramatic turnaround in our office in a short period of time, and she backed it up with our performance measures before and after I had taken charge.

Next up, the people we had helped. The press eventually got bored and left. (No juicy story of scandal, as they had been led to believe.) It turned out to be the best day of my entire tenure in DC government. I did not go home to Indiana. I stayed focused, and the department just kept getting better and better!

Build Relationships With Gatekeepers at Every Level

Administrative professionals, executive assistants, and department secretaries hold disproportionate access to information in any organization — and especially in political environments. These individuals often know the schedule, the strategy, and the sentiment long before it becomes official. Leaders who invest in genuine, respectful relationships with gatekeepers gain early intelligence, faster access, and allies in places that matter. In this case, a friendship between two executive assistants provided the intelligence that changed the outcome of a politically engineered attack.

When Someone Asks You to Keep a Secret That Protects Their Power, Refuse

Requests for confidentiality from people in authority — especially those asking you to take an action that compromises your integrity — are a form of coercion. The request itself is a warning sign. In high-stakes environments, the instinct to comply with authority must be overridden by the commitment to transparency and documentation. Never agree to a "private" conversation about a consequential matter without witnesses. Never accept a directive that you would be ashamed to defend publicly. If the request cannot withstand the light of day, it should not be honored.

Chapter 8
Investigations

"I smell a rat in this department."

It would have been too optimistic to think that the remaining troublemakers and misfits would give up on their quest to undermine our attempts at reform. After all, they had benefited from the chaos for years! It seemed like every month, the management team and I had to respond to a new investigation based on anonymous tips. There was the anonymous tip to the police department that there was a drug ring operating in the office. That was how I got to know the police chief well.

I cooperated fully with the police. The investigation was taken very seriously since there had been two overdoses in the office in quick succession of each other. I wanted to know more than anyone if it was true! Well, the investigation came up empty. There was NO evidence of a drug ring or of widespread drug usage in the office. Case closed.

After this investigation, I worked hard with the union to come up with a clear and concise drug policy for the department. It included referral to the employee assistance program for the first offense with suspension or termination for subsequent offenses. It was presented jointly by the union representative and me at a mandatory employee meeting with the opportunity for staff to ask questions and discuss the issue of drugs in the workplace. I could not say for sure that the policy worked except that we did not have any more drug overdoses in the department during my three-year tenure.

One of the troublemakers that remained in the office was a Bible-carrying, scripture-reciting evangelist. He would come in to work every day Bible in hand reciting his scripture for the day to anyone who would listen and then go in his office and shut and lock the door the rest of the day.

His job title was senior accountant which meant he made approximately $60,000 per year. I never saw anything he produced, so I finally asked Diane what he did. She told me that officially he was assigned to compiling and submitting the monthly financial reports to the mayor's office and subsequently to the federal government. Diane said that every month it was a fight to get him to do them and that they were never correct or on time, so she started doing them herself. I asked her how long she had been doing them and she said, "Almost since the day you started." That was unacceptable. It was not a hard concept. EVERYONE DOES THEIR JOB!

I set a meeting with Donald. In attendance were Diane, Donald, and I. Immediately after we were seated, he asked if we could pray before we began. I said yes. I then told him that the meeting was about his job description and performance. I asked if he wanted a union representative present. He said no. I asked him what his job duties were. He answered that he was assigned to do the monthly financial reports. I asked him had he been doing them. He went into a tirade about how he had trouble getting all the information required from the other managers.

I said, "Did you ask for help or bring it to my attention?"

He said NO. That was the truth. But then he added, "I found a way to get it done! Every one of them has been completed and turned in on time!"

To this day, I do not understand why he thought Diane would not have told me that she was doing the reports. Perhaps he thought that because he had known her longer than I had that she would not tell me.

I said "Donald, Diane has been doing the reports for nearly a year now. Do you think it's fair for her to do your job in addition to her own? Did you know she has been working overtime with no monetary compensation to do your job and hers?"

Silence.

I told him he was responsible for completing the reports himself effectively immediately. Also effective immediately, I would review them before they were submitted so the deadline for them would be moved one week earlier, so that I would have time for review. (The truth of the matter is accounting is not one of my strengths. But I had to interject myself in order to make HIM accountable.)

The meeting minutes, copies of each report with the due dates and penalties, if the due dates were not met, were all documented and given to him. The meeting was adjourned, and Donald started doing the reports.

Another investigation! Again, it was the DC inspector general's office. An anonymous tip with supporting documentation had been submitted to the DC inspector general's office claiming that I was misusing government funds because I did not consistently sign in when I arrived and sign out when I went home. Attached to this claim were copies of the department time sheets and MY pay stubs!

The allegation was that the days I did not sign in were days that I was absent from work, but my sick time or vacation time was never charged, and my pay was not docked. I would admit that I was not consistent in signing in and out. I had NEVER had to do it in any position I held before, and I was consumed (some would say obsessed) with getting the department turned around. I was working fifty to sixty hours a week, including many long hours at home and into the night. Well, this oversight led to a full-fledged investigation of ME!

What saved me was my habit of a to-do list every day, keeping a meticulous calendar and follow-up notes to every meeting, AND the fact that I did not ever throw them away! I had to turn over my calendar, to-do lists, and meeting notes to the inspector general dating back to the beginning of my tenure.

There was an abundance of evidence that I was at work every day that I had been paid and that I was getting things done! I also found out that it was Donald who had provided the anonymous tip and documentation.

Well, there was a cloud hanging over my head for several weeks while the inspector general completed the investigation; but eventually, CASE CLOSED. NO EVIDENCE OF MISUSE OF FUNDS. NO EVIDENCE OF ANY WRONG DOING! BUT WAIT! What about the "anonymous" tip and dubiously acquired evidence? I was told that there were grounds for me to file disciplinary action against Donald who had used his position to obtain my personal pay records. I chose not to do this. I felt it would look vindictive and self-serving. Donald claimed he knew God. I would let God handle it.

Documentation Is Your Most Valuable Leadership Asset

In high-accountability, high-conflict environments, the leader who survives is almost never the one with the best intentions — it is the one with the best records. Maintain a contemporaneous log of all significant decisions, directives given, employee interactions, disciplinary actions, and performance data. Store it systematically and keep it indefinitely. When an anonymous allegation or an Inspector General investigation arrives — and in toxic workplaces, it will — your documentation is your defense, your proof of performance, and your organizational legacy.

Assume Your Adversaries Are Playing a Long Game

Leaders in toxic organizations often make the mistake of believing that visible progress will neutralize opposition. It will not. Those who have built their careers on dysfunction often escalate their efforts precisely when threatened by improvement. Maintain your situational awareness. Continue to document. Continue to build external relationships. Effective leaders in hostile environments do not relax their guard after early wins — they build institutional resilience that can withstand sustained attack.

Chapter 9
The Noise Gets Too Loud!

As I began my third year in DC government, everything was going according to plan. The department staffing malaise had finally stabilized. I had put in place an excellent management team. We had passed the federal audits with ease avoiding any penalties, and our performance (tied to incentives) was improving steadily. Our partners: the court, the US marshal's office, the departments of vital records and economic development were extremely satisfied with our working relationship. My assessment was that, at last, we were a *normal* office. I had firm evidence of this when the following incident was relayed to me.

Two of the department's investigators got into a heated argument while in the office. It became so hot, in fact, that they were close to blows when one of them said, "Man! We better take this outside. I.J. will fire both of us if we don't stop! I need this job!"

Hearing this brought a smile to my lips. I had their respect, and they valued their jobs. They didn't fight, and they certainly didn't get fired.

BUT WAIT! The political pressure outside the office was heating up to a fever pitch.

It started with the public firing of three department heads that were hired around the same time as me. As a matter of fact, the four of us had formed an alliance and helped each other as we learned our way navigating the treacherous political waters of Washington DC.

I had seen all three of them coming out of a late meeting the day before. We spoke briefly; I was running late. In retrospect, they looked sad, but that was nothing new when you work in DC.

Every day was a different challenge: some days were happy, other days were sad.

The next morning, on the front page of Metro Section of the *Washington Post*, the headline was the firing of three DC government department heads for misuse of public funds! WHAT! The article alleged that all three were charging the government for their rent and living expenses more than twelve months after being hired. To this day, I did not know if it was true, but if it was, it could have only occurred if somebody within DC government approved it. I also knew that it was a dumb decision to think it was okay for the government to pay your rent.

The very public terminations immediately changed the way the government operated on a daily basis. Almost everyone became defensive, and there was an overreaction.

One example, for every expenditure, an additional form and approval was now required. This change was for everything from paper clips to major capital expenditures. Department heads had no individual discretion to spend money for anything even if the money was already earmarked for specific items. If something had been ordered but not delivered before the new executive policy took effect, the order had to be cancelled. It literally crippled agency operations.

I distinctly remember the first time I went into my purse for money to buy toilet tissue for the office. That was the pattern for several months!

There were also changes in the reporting structure. NO ONE reported directly to the Mayor's office anymore. No subordinate could even talk to Mayor Barry anymore.

Suddenly, he was surrounded by a wall of protection that was impenetrable even to those who he had worked closely with like me. Paranoia had really set in, and there was a different rumor flying within the walls of DC government every day. Speculation abounded as to who would be fired next. I could not get an answer to simple questions from the mayor's office. I no longer had a supervisor to go to with a problem. I remember being grateful that this was not the atmosphere when I started three years ago. Jennifer would be in charge!

Every day the headlines in the DC papers Metro Section outlined a new infraction, a new allegation. Mayor Barry was the target. He was having an affair. He was misusing funds. He was on drugs. He was unfit to continue. He had bribed officials. He had taken bribes. He was a terrible husband.

He was a terrible father. He stole gasoline! It was the most incredible and disheartening thing I had ever witnessed, and few, if any of the accusations, were substantiated with hard evidence.

Employees were frustrated and started acting out. I had to develop a new strategy quickly to weather this political nightmare.

After consulting with those close to me, I decided that my new course of action would be to strengthen my relationship and alliance with the federal government. They knew me. More importantly, they knew the journey (upwards) that my department had traveled. They were a formidable third party that also had a vested interest in my department's operations and continuing success. If the wild lies and accusations permeating some DC government departments, eventually were directed our way the Feds could be a truth teller about me and my department. Thankfully, it never came to that, but it always pays to have a contingency plan!

The next eventful headline was the arrest of one of Mayor Barry's top aides for embezzlement. On the heels of that came the resignation of the city administrator. The government was falling apart, and it did not appear that there was anyone left who was credible to speak on the government's behalf.

The rumors continued to run rampant. No one seemed to know the government's position on anything. I tried to continue business as usual, but everywhere I went outside the department, I was asked questions about Mayor Barry and the headlines. I remember one time after I delivered the keynote address at a conference (and I nailed that speech), when the floor was opened for questions, NOT ONE PERSON asked a question about the subject of my presentation. Every question was about Mayor Barry. The final question asked was "How can you work for a man like that?"

This is how I answered:

> I base my assessment of people on how they treat me personally and professionally. I cannot speak to the actions of anyone outside my personal interactions and experience with them. Mayor Barry has been nothing but supportive of me and my department. You all know where we started, and you just heard where we are now. None of it would have been possible without the leadership and support I have known with this mayor. He had a big role in the success we've had, and I will never say a bad word about him.

> (Drop the mic!)

But things continued to get worse. I could not go in or out of my office without being hounded by press. I could not even attend nongovernment events without constantly being stopped by people asking me questions about Mayor

Barry. What made things worse was that even midlevel employees were also cornered by reporters and asked to give statements and personal explanations for what was going on inside DC government. Many of them were influenced by the spotlight, eager to have their fifteen minutes of fame, and many said things they should not have said. It was a true circus.

The last shoe finally dropped. Mayor Barry was indicted as the result of a drug sting, and he resigned. I felt like a member of my family had died. When I did not think it could get any worse, it did. Suddenly, there was no one in charge. Nobody would (or could) tell us what was happening and/or how we should conduct business. There was not even the general directive of "if approached by the press, refer them to the public relations person." I did not know who the public relations person was. He or she certainly kept a low profile!

A couple of days after his indictment, Mayor Barry addressed all of the employees. It was a pep talk, an introduction of the acting chain of command and a goodbye speech. There was not a dry eye among the employees. Mayor Barry had an in-depth knowledge of the entire DC government. He could tell you every detail from the process for filing for section eight housing to the emergency procedures in case of a terrorist attack. He knew where you should go to file for Medicaid, and he could give you a quick lesson on how to boot a car for a parking violation. His real gift as a politician was his ability to remember the names of every person he met and to make you feel like a good friend. In fact, he knew most of the 1,500 or so employees by name. Not only that, if you told him something personal about you, he would remember that too. He had a photographic memory and he was brilliant. But now, all that was over! He talked to all of the district's employees, and then he faced the press.

I was in my third year of employment when Mayor Barry resigned.

Build a Contingency Plan Before Your Chain of Command Changes

Leadership transitions — whether through resignation, termination, reorganization, or political upheaval — are among the most dangerous periods for an organization that has been in turnaround. Effective leaders anticipate this risk and establish independent sources of support, credibility, and authority before they are needed. Identify stakeholders who have witnessed your performance and who exist outside the chain of command that is at risk. These relationships become your institutional anchors when the organizational structure dissolves.

Do Not Attach Your Career to Any Single Leader

Sponsorship from a powerful executive can accelerate a leader's trajectory significantly — but it also creates dangerous dependency. When your sponsor falls, you fall with them unless you have developed independent credibility. The most durable leaders build reputations that transcend any single relationship: results that speak for themselves, external visibility, documented performance, and relationships that span organizational boundaries. Sponsor relationships are assets. They should never become the foundation of your professional identity.

Chapter 10
Bureaucracy Reigns!

"I.J., tell me again what your department does and how this federal funding stuff works."

That was my world after Mayor Barry resigned. Educating the new administration, most of which had never worked in government and many of which had never managed an organization before. I was reasonably sure some could not even manage a household budget, let alone one of the DC government's size and magnitude!

I remember spending eight hours one day briefing the new members of the administration only to have some of them resign the next week. Meaning, I had to do the same thing all over again.

A new organizational chart was circulated weekly and where my department was going to land was a wide-open question. Prior to Mayor Barry's resignation, we had been an *independent* department reporting directly to the mayor's office. With the generous federal funding plus the performance incentives we generated, our budget was covered one hundred percent! There was also money left over to help fund other parts of the DC government.

Then someone in the new administration decided that ALL federal funding and incentives we generated should go to the general fund and we should "get in line" for our administrative budget just like everybody else. They also said since we were doing so well, we could stand to have our budget cut! They did not understand how a federal matching program worked:

For every dollar the DC government contributed, the federal government would match it with two dollars. But for every dollar of administrative funding that was cut, the DC government LOST two dollars. Now, I understand politics, and I agree that the city's priority should be the basic city services—public safety (police and fire departments), health, and education, and even making sure the trash gets picked up and the streets are repaired—but this move said to me, "Work as hard as you can. Generate all the federal dollars you can. But neither you or your office will benefit in any way from your hard work!" It was a devastating blow!

Despite the complexity and unique characteristics, my department no longer enjoyed the independence and autonomy we once had, and we no longer reported directly to the mayor's office. Honestly, I understand this decision. It made sense. I reported directly to Mayor Barry the prior three years because of the mess the department was in at the time I was hired. It was necessary to remove the bureaucratic barriers that would have delayed and impeded the kind of drastic, rapid, and positive changes that needed to occur, but the new administration decided my department should be buried deep in human services with welfare, food stamps, and foster care. BUT WAIT. My department generated revenue, so it should be housed in internal revenue. BUT WAIT. We worked closely with the court, and US marshals and our legal staff were essentially civil prosecutors, so should not we be housed in the attorney general's office or the corporation counsel's office?

I was growing weary. I had spent my time and energy for three years building something positive. Now my time and energy were being spent assisting (or resisting) the bureaucratization of the substantially autonomous and highly successful department that I had been permitted and encouraged to build!

The final insult in this bureaucratic maze was that the number of reports we needed to prepare and submit weekly quadrupled. This was in addition to the monthly, quarterly, and annual federal reports. We were drowning in reporting deadlines. Office supplies were counted. Truly, the number of boxes of paper clips and copier paper were tallied and doled out to the departments like it was gold!

Department heads like me had to devise *schemes* to get the supplies needed to perform daily duties. I knew the time had come for me to leave when I was absolutely jubilant to hear we had received a shipment of copier paper!

BUT WAIT, I. J.! WHAT DID I JUST SAY!

This was an actual light bulb moment. I was overjoyed at what should have been a mundane event! It was time to leave.

Audit Where Your Time Goes — Especially When Bureaucracy Expands

In bureaucratic environments, compliance and reporting demands expand to fill available leadership capacity. If left unchecked, an executive's days become entirely consumed by internal process rather than meaningful outcomes. Conduct a regular, honest assessment of how you are spending your time. If the majority of your energy is going toward administrative compliance, internal politics, or low-stakes decisions that should be delegated, you are experiencing scope erosion. Address it directly, or recognize that the role has changed in ways that no longer align with your strengths.

Recognize Your Own Inflection Points — and Act On Them

The most dangerous career trap for high-achieving leaders is the slow normalization of diminished expectations. When you find yourself celebrating what was once unremarkable — a supply delivery, a routine approval, a week without a crisis — your internal bar has shifted. These moments are not failures; they are data. They tell you that the environment has imposed its ceiling on your ambitions. The leaders who thrive over long careers pay close attention to these inflection points and treat them as legitimate signals to recalibrate, reset, or move on.

Organizational Pressure Is Not Permission to Abandon Your Standards

One of the most insidious effects of sustained chaos is the way it gradually reframes mediocrity as achievement. Leaders who survive toxic environments must maintain a parallel internal standard — one that is immune to organizational pressure and anchored to their own definition of excellence. This is not rigidity; it is identity. The moment you measure success by what the organization tolerates rather than what you know is possible, you have begun to lead on the organization's terms rather than your own.

Chapter 11

Are You in a Toxic Workplace?
A Self-Assessment for Leaders

Every story in this book began the same way: with a leader walking into an organization that looked one way from the outside and was something entirely different on the inside. One of the most dangerous things about toxic workplaces is how hey normalize themselves. The longer you are inside them, the more their dysfunction starts to feel like just the way things are.

I have worked decades consulting for, and speaking about organizational culture — from government agencies to Fortune 500 boardrooms. The questions I am asked most often by leaders at every level are some version of the same thing: Is this normal? Is it me? Is it them? How do I know when it is truly toxic — and when is it just hard?

This chapter is my answer. It is a structured self-assessment designed for leaders — managers, directors, executives, and anyone responsible for the performance and well-being of a team. It is not a clinical instrument. It is the distilled wisdom of someone who has lived these experiences, learned from them, and watched what happens when leaders fail to name what they are dealing with.

Complete both parts honestly. The assessment is only useful if you resist the temptation to answer the way you wish things were rather than the way they actually are.

PART ONE: ASSESSING YOUR ENVIRONMENT

For each statement below, score yourself honestly: 0 = Never, 1 = Occasionally, 2 = Often, 3 = Consistently.

#	Statement	Scale	Score	Notes
A. Leadership & Management Behavior				
1.	My supervisor or senior leaders are unpredictable — their moods or standards change without explanation.	0 1 2 3	___	
2.	Credit for successes is claimed by leadership; blame for failures is redirected to staff.	0 1 2 3	___	
3.	Decisions are made without transparency, consultation, or clear rationale.	0 1 2 3	___	
4.	Political connections or personal relationships determine who is protected and who is held accountable.	0 1 2 3	___	
5.	Leaders respond to legitimate concerns with retaliation, silence, or dismissal.	0 1 2 3	___	
B. Team & Interpersonal Dynamics				
6.	Gossiping, rumor-spreading, or character assassination is a routine feature of office culture.	0 1 2 3	___	
7.	Staff members are afraid to voice disagreement, raise concerns, or ask questions.	0 1 2 3	___	
8.	Cliques and alliances divide the team, creating insiders and outsiders.	0 1 2 3	___	
9.	Bullying, intimidation, or verbal aggression is tolerated by management.	0 1 2 3	___	
10.	High-performing employees are isolated, undermined, or driven out.	0 1 2 3	___	

C. Accountability & Performance

11.	Employees who do little or nothing suffer no meaningful consequences.	0 1 2 3	___
12.	Performance standards are applied inconsistently — some staff are held accountable while others are protected.	0 1 2 3	___
13.	Disciplinary processes are used as weapons rather than as legitimate management tools.	0 1 2 3	___
14.	Results and outcomes matter less than appearances, politics, or relationships.	0 1 2 3	___
15.	Good work is neither recognized nor rewarded in any meaningful way.	0 1 2 3	___

D. Organizational Structure & Communication

16.	Policies and procedures are unclear, inconsistently enforced, or routinely ignored.	0 1 2 3	___
17.	Important information is withheld, distorted, or weaponized.	0 1 2 3	___
18.	The chain of command is unreliable — going around it is necessary to get anything done.	0 1 2 3	___
19.	Bureaucratic obstacles prevent even reasonable decisions from being made efficiently.	0 1 2 3	___
20.	The organization responds to external pressure or crisis by tightening control rather than improving function.	0 1 2 3	___

E. Your Personal Experience

21.	I find myself dreading coming to work in ways that feel qualitatively different from normal stress.	0 1 2 3	___
22.	I have adjusted my standards downward to survive in this environment.	0 1 2 3	___
23.	I spend significant mental energy on self-protection rather than on productive work.	0 1 2 3	___
24.	I feel isolated — without allies, mentors, or colleagues I can trust.	0 1 2 3	___
25.	I recognize that my health, relationships, or self-confidence are being affected by this environment.	0 1 2 3	___

PART ONE TOTAL SCORE (out of 75): __________

PART ONE: SCORING GUIDE

Score Range	Classification	What It Means & What to Do
0 – 15	**Healthy Environment**	Dysfunction exists — it always does — but it is isolated and manageable. Your organization has functional structures, reasonable accountability, and a culture that supports performance. Continue to build the relationships and documentation habits that protect you if conditions change.
16 – 30	**Stressed but Functional**	Significant dysfunction is present in multiple areas. The environment is not yet irreparably toxic, but without deliberate intervention — better accountability structures, leadership development, or external support — it will worsen. Identify the two or three highest-scoring areas and build a focused improvement plan.
31 – 45	**Dysfunctional**	You are operating in a seriously dysfunctional environment. Chronic stress, political interference, and accountability failures are degrading performance and culture. This is the environment I.J. Neal walked into in Washington, DC. Immediate, structural intervention is required — and you must determine honestly whether you have the authority and support to deliver it.
46 – 60	**Toxic**	The environment is toxic. Individual coping strategies will not be sufficient. The culture is actively causing harm to individuals and to organizational performance. If you are a leader in this environment, your first obligation is to protect your team, document everything, and escalate to every available authority. If escalation is not possible, the most important decision you face is whether to stay.
61 – 75	**Severely Toxic / Crisis**	This environment meets every clinical and organizational definition of a toxic workplace in crisis. Physical safety, mental health, and professional integrity are all at risk. If you are a leader here, you must activate every external resource available to you — legal counsel, HR, regulatory bodies, federal oversight — and you must seriously evaluate whether your continued presence is sustainable or strategic.

PART TWO: THE LEADER'S MIRROR

This section asks the harder questions — the ones most leaders avoid. A toxic workplace is not only defined by what is happening around you. It is also defined by what you are doing, allowing, and becoming inside it.

Answer each question as honestly as you can. There is no score here. These are reflection questions — the kind I had to ask myself more than once during my three years in DC.

Reflection Question	My Honest Answer
YOUR STANDARDS	
1.1 Have I lowered my performance expectations — for myself or my team — to match what the environment tolerates rather than what I know is possible? *(See: Chapter 10 — the copier paper moment.)*	
1.2 Am I celebrating outcomes I once would have considered inadequate?	
1.3 When did I last accomplish something I was genuinely proud of?	
YOUR INTEGRITY	
2.1 Have I ever been asked — explicitly or implicitly — to overlook wrongdoing, protect a connected employee, or stay silent about something I know is wrong? *(See: Chapter 7 — the Councilman's call.)*	
2.2 Have I complied with any of those requests?	
2.3 Is there anything happening in my department right now that I would be unwilling to defend publicly?	
YOUR RELATIONSHIPS	
3.1 Have I built genuine, reciprocal relationships with stakeholders outside my immediate chain of command — people who would show up for me if I needed them? *(See: Chapter 1 — the show of force.)*	

3.2	Am I dependent on a single sponsor or political relationship for my safety in this organization? *(See: Chapter 9 — Mayor Barry's fall.)*
3.3	Do I have at least one colleague I can speak to with complete candor about what is happening?
YOUR PEOPLE	
4.1	Is there someone on my team experiencing something I know about but have not addressed — bullying, substance abuse, mental health crisis — because addressing it feels too difficult? *(See: Chapters 4 and 5.)*
4.2	Am I protecting my best people from the environment, or am I allowing the environment to erode them?
4.3	If my best employee were offered a role elsewhere today, would they take it?
YOUR FUTURE	
5.1	Can I articulate a clear vision for what this organization will look like in twelve months, and do I believe it is achievable?
5.2	Do I have the authority, resources, and support required to achieve the outcomes I was hired to deliver? *(See: Chapter 2 — setting the table for success.)*
5.3	If I am honest with myself — is it time to leave? *(See: Chapter 10 — knowing when the chapter has closed.)*

What To Do With Your Results

The value of this assessment is not in the number. It is in the honesty. Most leaders in toxic workplaces already know — on some level — what the environment is doing to them, their teams, and their results. What they lack is the language, the framework, and sometimes the permission to name it clearly and act accordingly.

Here is what I know from experience:

01	**Name It**	You cannot address what you will not name. If the assessment reflects a toxic or dysfunctional environment, say so — to yourself first, then to at least one trusted colleague or advisor. Leaders who reframe dysfunction as "just how it is here" or "the price of the role" are making a choice to absorb the damage without confronting the cause.
02	**Document Everything**	Start immediately. Decisions made, directives given, incidents witnessed, conversations held. Date everything. Keep copies in a location outside the organization's control. In toxic workplaces, documentation is not paranoia — it is professional survival. It is also how you protect the people who work for you.
03	**Build Your Coalition**	Identify the external stakeholders who have a vested interest in your department's success. Federal partners, regulatory agencies, professional associations, elected officials who benefit from your results. Cultivate those relationships before you need them. They are your leverage — and your protection — when the internal environment turns against you.
04	**Protect Your Best People**	The first casualties of a toxic environment are always the highest performers. They have the most options, the lowest tolerance for dysfunction, and the clearest view of what is happening. If you do not actively shield your best people from the worst of the culture, you will lose them — and you will deserve to. Retaining excellence in a toxic environment requires deliberate, consistent effort.
05	**Decide Your Terms**	Staying in a toxic environment is a legitimate choice — sometimes the most courageous one available. But it must be a conscious, strategic choice made on your terms, not a passive slide into accommodation. Decide what you are willing to do and what you are not. Decide what outcomes will signal that the work is done or that the cost has become too high. Know your exit conditions before the environment decides them for you.

"Leading in chaos is not about being fear-less. It is about being clear — about who you are, what you stand for, and what you will and will not accept. That clarity is what gets you through."

Epilogue

"I.J., this is Mr. Cane, senior vice president at IBM Corporation. We've heard about you and the good work you've done during your tenure in DC. We are starting a new initiative in our government services practice, and I wondered if you would be interested in coming in for an interview."

I said, "How about in fifteen minutes!"

I knew I had the job before the interview concluded.

Corporate America here I come!

Show them what you are made of, girl!

Excellence Is the Most Durable Career Strategy

Leaders who spend their careers navigating chaos, managing political threats, and delivering results in hostile environments often emerge with something that cannot be manufactured: a reputation built on verified performance. You do not need to self-promote when results speak for themselves. Pursue excellence in your current role — not as a means to an end, but as a standard of professional integrity. The opportunities will come. They always do.

SECTION 2

Onyx Rising Page
for Leading in Chaos
(Revised Edition)

The Frameworks in This Book
Are Just the Beginning

If the principles in Leading in Chaos resonated with you—the CHAOS Framework, the leadership insights, the hard questions about your own leadership—you already know that reading about change and actually leading it are two very different things.

Onyx Rising exists to bridge that gap.

We are a leadership and financial wellness consulting firm that works directly with organizations navigating disruption, dysfunction, and change. Our engagements are hands-on, customized, and build around your specific people—not a template.

Whether you are a CEO looking to transform your leadership culture, an HR Director building a financial wellness benefit, or a conference organizer seeking a keynote that moves people to action—we'd love to talk.

SERVICES:

Leading in Chaos: Leadership Development & Organizational Transformation

Money Matters: Image vs Reality® Financial Wellness for the Workforce

Keynotes & Speaking Engagements | Executive Coaching | Workshop Facilitation

Your organization deserves leaders who rise—even in chaos.

Start the conversation: www.onyx2rise.com/contact

Irma Neal, CEO & Co-Founder | Kelli Lester, Cofounder & Leadership Strategy Partner

Onyx Rising | onyx2rise.com

Acknowledgments

As I think back on all the people who helped me during the times outlined in this book, I could not have survived without a strong group of supporters and my faith. First, my father instilled in me the belief that there is no such word as "can't" and my mother taught me to always strive to "get an understanding". I would like to thank my long time friends, Carolyn and Bob, for editing the book. Thanks to the first author in the family, my daughter-in-law, for all her tips that were invaluable. I would like to thank my sisters for being a sounding board and supporting me during the trying journey to get the book published. Thanks to all the DC staff that helped me turn around the agency and did an outstanding job without individual recognition.

Thanks to my nephew Greg for his social media expertise. Thanks to Donna. This book would not have been possible without her. She is the one who convinced me to accept the DC position and the one who listened and advised me during all the chaos. I will be forever grateful for her support. Thanks to Diane, the person who lived the day-to-day chaos with me and became my best friend for life. Lastly, thanks to my one and only son, Willie. He is the one who keeps me looking forward and upward.

The journey of writing Leading in Chaos is bittersweet because it was done without my best friend, my soul mate, my love, my husband for 47 years, Sam. He said: "I will be right back." But he did not return. A reckless driver took his life and turned my world from bright to gray. All that I am and all that I do is dedicated to the love that Sam and I shared.

About the Author

I. J. Neal is a leadership strategist, Certified Financial Coach, and the CEO and Co-Founder of Onyx Rising LLC — a women-owned leadership and financial empowerment consulting firm she founded with her niece and business partner, Kelli Lester, in 2016.

Her career spans more than four decades of proven leadership in government, Corporate America, and entrepreneurship. As a department director for the District of Columbia she inherited one of the most dysfunctional agencies in city government and transformed it into one of the nation's top-performing programs — moving from 52nd to 10th on the federal performance scale in under three years. The stories and leadership frameworks in this book were forged in that experience.

She went on to serve as Vice President at IBM Corporation, where she helped grow the human services portfolio from zero to more than $200 million in three years. She co-founded and later sold Service Design Associates for millions. She served as Deputy Mayor of Indianapolis, Indiana, and as Vice President for Strategic Initiatives at the Center for the Support of Families. She has founded and sold four businesses and holds MWBE certification.

Through Onyx Rising, I. J. delivers two flagship programs: Leading in Chaos — a leadership development and organizational transformation program built on the C.H.A.O.S. Framework introduced in this book — and Money Matters: Image vs. Reality®, a federally registered financial wellness program designed to help working adults build financial stability and generational wealth.

She speaks nationally to executives, government leaders, and conference audiences on leading through disruption, building high-performance cultures, and navigating the real chaos that frameworks alone cannot prepare you for.

Learn more at www.onyx2rise.com

www.ingramcontent.com/pod-product-compliance
Lightning Source LLC
Chambersburg PA
CBHW031145250726
48655CB00002B/839